LAVERNE,

the Runway
Stowaway

by Judy McSweeney illustrated by Sharon Gonzales

"Kee-ZINK!"

The furry hairs on Jet's forehead stood straight up. What was that strange sound?
It startled him just as he was settling in for an afternoon doggy nap in his canine carrier.

"I wish I could run and jump and chase whatever is making that noise," he thought.

All he could do was roll a big brown eyeball toward that mysterious sound. "Maybe when SkyKid Sam
lets me out of this carrier, I can track it down."

Sam heard his eager pup whimpering and scratching. "What's the matter, boy? You know dogs can't run around
the airfield, even if your name *is* Jet!"

"That's a good one, Sam," laughed Propeller Pete as he steadied himself on the bumpy tram tour ride around the airfield.

Flygirl Pearl patted the top of the canine carrier. "It won't be long, Jet. Take it easy."

VRRROOOMMM!

Airfield tram rides are fun and they're the best way for visitors to see airplanes up close, but the planes sure are LOUD!

How can a sleepy dog take a nap when an airplane takes off or lands every other minute?

"Kee-ZINK!" "There's that noise again," Jet mumbled. It sure wasn't one of his friends, the Airport Explorers: SkyKid Sam, Propeller Pete, or Flygirl Pearl. They all make human noises. Jet's favorite sounds were Pearl's giggles and hums, Pete's whistles and toe-taps, and Sam . . . well, Sam liked to laugh out loud and make silly sounds that are only funny to a 12-year-old and his playful pup.

Together, they all have great fun at San Diego International Airport. Usually, kids and dogs can't roam around an airport and airfield, but the Airport Explorers, including Jet, had practically grown up here.

At least it seemed that way. Pearl's dad worked as a ticket agent and her mom was a pilot; Pete's mom was a tour guide and his dad was an airline mechanic and Sam's mom worked in airport operations and his dad was on the ramp crew. As for Jet, his background was a bit more questionable. . . .

All anyone knows is that he suddenly popped up one day, turning around and around on the baggage claim belt!

Sam's dad spotted him first and hollered for help. Soon, all the airport employees were chasing the dirty dizzy dog!

"This place is fun!" thought the furry mutt, as he zig-zagged past stern security officers, frustrated flight attendants, and puzzled passengers.

Suddenly, the playful pooch spotted Sam and leaped into his outstretched arms. Sam tumbled and rolled around giggling with his silly new friend.

"In for a safe landing!" grinned Sam, as he hugged his affectionate new pal. "Can I keep him, Dad? He's as fast as a jet!"

Sam's dad explained that he probably had a home and that someone would be looking for him, but no one ever came.

Soon "Jet" was named and claimed and cleaned and screened.

That's the exciting day Jet became an official Airport Explorer, with three new fun friends—Sam, Pete, and Pearl.

But today, sitting in his carrier and staring out the little air-hole window wasn't so fun.

"Kee-ZINK!"

There's that sound again!

At last the tour tram ride squealed to a safe stop and the wide-eyed tour-takers carefully stepped off the vehicle's platform.

"Yea!" thought Jet as his tail wagged in anticipation of freedom.

"Kee-ZINK! Kee-ZINK!"

Now Jet was really worried, or at least as worried as a dog can get. What was that strange sound coming from his tail?

"Oh, no!" he said to himself.

Jet spun in a fast half-circle, trying desperately to catch the end of his own wiggling tip. It didn't work. He only managed to wedge himself backward in his carrier, with his hind end sticking out the front window and his nose nestled deep in the dark.

Something tickled his whiskers. . . .

"Kee-ZINK!"

"Who's there?" Jet barked in a low growl, trying to sound as frightening as he could.

"I'm Laverne," came the tiny reply.

Startled and scared, Jet tried to back away, but he only managed to shove his tail tighter into the open air-hole window until it was almost stuck!

"Laverne, the least tern . . . actually, a California least tern. I can help you get your tail out—or is that how it's supposed to be?"

5

"Huh? Who? What?" was all that Jet could sputter.

He tried to regain his canine composure, but he wasn't sure whether to be afraid of his intruder or excited at the idea of making a new friend.

"Whoever you are, please, oh please, don't be a predator," declared Laverne.

"Uh, okay," wagged the confused pup. "I'm called Jet and I'm a dog. I'm supposed to be a hunter, but don't worry, I won't hurt you—I promise. What's a least tern and what are you doing in HERE?" he blurted.

Of course, San Diego International Airport was in San Diego, California, but after that, Jet couldn't make sense of this crazy bird who claimed to be a California least tern.

"Let's go, boy!" shouted Sam, and the furry and feathered new friends jostled from side to side as Sam grabbed the carrier and ran into the airport terminal.

Pearl was humming happily. "I love to ride along with your mom's tours, Pete," she said as she smiled and waved goodbye to the tourists. "I always see something new on the airfield."

"You sure got THAT right," thought Jet, as he tried to focus in the dark on his newfound companion. He sniffed her soft feathers.

"Your whiskers TICKLE!" tittered Laverne, as she fluttered her wing on Jet's soggy snout.

"ACHOO!" blew Jet, as the silky feathers rippled over his moist muzzle. The wispy feathers wafted straight up before falling softly back into place.

They stared at each other for a moment then suddenly burst into giggles, sounding like two old friends.

"I'm on a secret mission," blurted out Laverne bravely, just as Sam unlatched the carrier door. She whispered quickly, "Will you please help me, Jet?"

Jet thought quickly and lifted a big floppy ear. Laverne took the cue and leaped under the furry flap and held on, just as Jet pattered out of the carrier to follow Sam.

As soon as the group made their way to the airport terminal operations office, Jet quickly slipped into a hiding spot behind Sam's backpack. He shook his head until Laverne plopped out.

In the bright light of the office, Jet could see his stowaway more clearly.

Two stubby orange legs, looking like skinny carrots on webbed clawed feet, stuck out boldly from a ball of fluffy feathers. A snowy white face, neck, and belly were surrounded by rainstorm-gray wings. A sunset yellow bill was centered in the middle of the whole package.

But the most striking characteristic was a BLACK MASK!

The mask of a bandit!

A feathery bandit. With wings. And a beak.

The whole top of her head was black. She looked like she was wearing a burglar hat. A black mask-like stripe ran across her eyes to the beak, revealing a stark white patch of forehead in between.

"Are you wearing a mask because you're on a secret mission?" asked Jet, fascinated by his mysterious new companion.

"Perhaps," came her peculiar reply.

7

Jet had a lot more questions to ask but he could see that Laverne was no longer paying attention. She was too busy tilting her dark masked eyes to see around the operations room.

"Where are we?" Laverne whispered.

"Airside Operations," said Jet proudly. "This is where you can get a bird's eye view of the airfield and watch the minute-to-minute action on the airstrip."

"Bird's eye view?" questioned the intrigued tern.

"Yes, actually," smiled Jet, staring out the gigantic window overlooking the runway. Below, he could see the huge airplanes taking turns taking off and landing. Some were getting serviced by the fuel trucks. Others were getting luggage loaded into their bellies.

"The mission of the humans that work in Operations is to make sure everyone and everything on the airfield is safe and secure, and that every flight is running smoothly," said Jet.

"EVERY flight?" questioned Laverne.

Jet glanced at his curious playmate.

"Of course," Jet replied. "So, Laverne . . . what's *your* mission?"

Laverne looked Jet up and down and from side to side.

"Can you keep a secret?" she chirped quietly.

Jet leaned in closely.

"Kee-ZINK!"

"Why did you do THAT?" Jet sputtered as he stumbled backward.

"Someone is coming!" insisted Laverne, as she jumped behind Sam's backpack.

"Let's explore Operations for a while before we get started," said Sam, as he walked by Jet and over toward the window to enjoy the view of the airfield.

But Sam's friends didn't know that today's adventure would be very different from their typical airport operations . . . and Sam didn't know that the Airport Explorers would be carrying a very different kind of passenger.

Meanwhile, Jet worried about his strange new friend. Laverne must have snuck into his carrier during the tram tour. Did she come from the airfield? Is she in danger?

Jet looked her straight in one of her masked eyeballs and firmly commanded, "Okay, tell me everything."

"All right," agreed Laverne.

She began her amazing story.

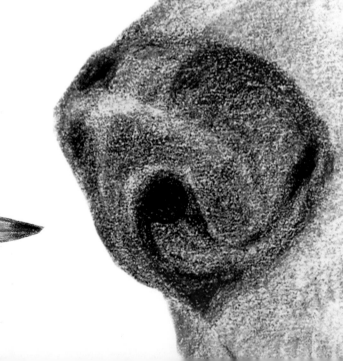

"My real name is Sterna antillarum browni but you can call me 'Laverne' because that means 'born in the spring' and well, I was."

Jet shifted nervously. He wondered what he had gotten himself into.

"So what does 'least tern' mean?" he ventured.

"'The least' means 'the smallest.' I'm the smallest of the North American tern family—that's a type of bird."

"Are you a bandit?" Jet had to ask.

"No, silly, but I am endangered," explained Laverne.

"What's endangered?" asked Jet.

"I'm not sure," she admitted. "I once heard my parents discussing it. They also said to watch out for predators."

Now Jet became even more nervous about this new mysterious creature. This endangered bird with PARENTS . . . could she be trouble?

Suddenly, Jet realized that Laverne, no matter who she was, would probably be missed and that her parents would be worried. He knew he had to get this little bird back to her home soon, wherever that was!

Jet continued his interrogation. "Where did you come from?"

"An egg," revealed Laverne.

Jet rolled his eyes. Of course birds come from eggs. "But where was your egg when you hatched?" he continued, trying to zone in on the location of Laverne's origins.

"In a nest," Laverne answered.

"WHERE IS YOUR NEST?!?" groaned Jet.

"In a little shallow hole beside the runway!"

"Runway? What runway?" Jet yipped in a panicked bark.

"Why, at the end of Runway 27, of course!" Laverne said proudly.

Now this was starting to make a little sense to Jet. Runway 27 is the airstrip at San Diego International Airport. The tour tram was riding beside it when Laverne first "Kee-ZINKed" into Jet's life.

"What? Why would you live on the runway? How . . . and why did you end up in my carrier, and why do you make that Kee-ZINK sound?" continued Jet, trying to get as many questions answered as possible.

"That's where all our nests are! My folks say the noise of the planes keeps away those predators they're worried about. Anyway, I was just hanging out in the neighborhood, and well, I was practicing for my mission."

"What IS your mission?" asked Jet, remembering his earlier question was never answered.

"I want to fly," exclaimed Laverne in her biggest voice Jet had heard yet. "I can't."

"Don't say you can't," encouraged Jet. "Just say, 'I'm working on it.'"

"Okay," hesitated Laverne. "Well, I'm working on flying, and that's what I was doing when a big wind swept me into this huge moving thing on wheels. I was so scared I started to chirp "Kee-ZINK" to call my mom, but the ride kept moving and I pushed through a small hole in your carrier to hide from all the big shoes."

Jet smiled, thinking of all the shoes the tourists were wearing that morning on the tram vehicle.

"So, here I am," sighed Laverne. "I want to go home, but I should bring a souvenir for my mother. And by the way, I'm getting hungry," she finished.

Jet was beginning to get the whole picture. He realized he was going to have to help adventurous little Laverne get back to her nest. But how? The next tram tour ride was not until next week, and he sure wasn't allowed to go on the airfield alone. Jet also realized he had no clue what least terns eat.

"What do you eat?" asked Jet. He had heard the phrase *she eats like a bird*, and now he wished he knew exactly what was on that bird-like menu.

"Oh, I like topsmelt!" offered Laverne.

"Is that some kind of sandwich?" pondered Jet aloud.

Laverne shook with laughter. "No, that's a fish, but I'll settle for northern anchovy, jacksmelt, California killifish, walleye surfperch, shiner perch . . . oh, almost any kind of fish will do—I'm not picky."

Jet was really worried now. He had been to the bay beside the airport, but he had never caught a fish!

13

"Yikes, let's hurry," shouted Sam, "or we'll be late!" Jet nudged Laverne into Sam's backpack just as Pete let out a powerful whistle. At Pete's signal, the Airport Explorers grabbed their backpacks and headed into the terminal. They looked a lot like the busy traveling passengers hurrying to catch their flights. But the Airport Explorers weren't going on a plane today. They had a different kind of destination to visit.

Jet scampered beside his pals while Laverne slid down between the papers, books, snacks, and other supplies in Sam's backpack.

"What's this?" she wondered as she discovered a package at the bottom of the backpack. Curious Laverne pecked it open. "What a delicious smell!" She could not resist it and began to nibble.

"Gooey and sticky, yum!" grinned Laverne. "This sure isn't fish! What great discoveries I am making on this mission!"

This reminded her that she hadn't yet completed her mission to fly and that made her sad. Then she remembered what Jet had taught her.

"I AM working on flying," she boldly announced through a mouthful of thick goo. "But first," she said, "I'm going to work on whatever this tasty thing is!" And she gobbled it up!

After a while, Laverne didn't feel well. Her tummy felt funny and her feathers were sticky. She was beginning to miss her parents and she still had not accomplished her mission.

Laverne curled up in the bottom of the backpack and soon fell fast asleep.

Jet was panting as he and his three friends (well, four if you count Laverne) entered the office marked

ENVIRONMENTAL AFFAIRS DEPARTMENT.

The Airport Explorers had been there before, helping out with recycling and other environmental projects at the airport. But today, the airport's Environmental Affairs Department was working with Mayra, a wildlife biologist. She promised the Airport Explorers a new adventure, and they couldn't wait to get started.

"What's our mission today, Mayra?" Sam asked as he watched her pack unusual equipment and supplies into two small tool boxes.

Laverne woke up at the word "mission." She realized she felt much better and carefully stepped out of the backpack so she could listen to Mayra's mission explanation.

"Today we are . . ."

"What do you have all OVER you?" Jet yapped.

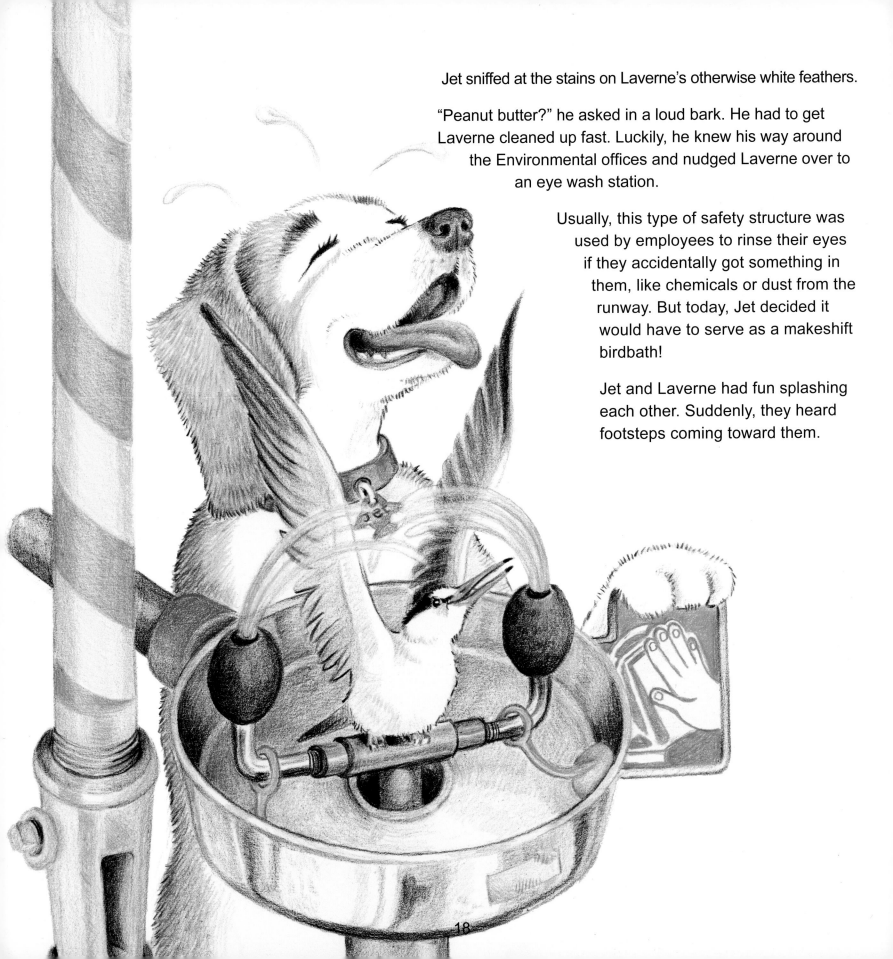

Jet sniffed at the stains on Laverne's otherwise white feathers.

"Peanut butter?" he asked in a loud bark. He had to get Laverne cleaned up fast. Luckily, he knew his way around the Environmental offices and nudged Laverne over to an eye wash station.

Usually, this type of safety structure was used by employees to rinse their eyes if they accidentally got something in them, like chemicals or dust from the runway. But today, Jet decided it would have to serve as a makeshift birdbath!

Jet and Laverne had fun splashing each other. Suddenly, they heard footsteps coming toward them.

"Yikes, this looks like trouble," thought Jet.

"Now that you're clean, get back in here fast," Jet whispered as he lifted his ear up, off the right side of his face.

Laverne slid under Jet's warm fluffy ear, which was perfectly suited for drying and warming her wet feathers.

"You mean 'in EAR?'" Laverne quipped back.

"Smart aleck!" Jet smiled.

"Thanks," Laverne grinned back.

"Where'd you go, boy? We're taking off!" shouted Sam as he jogged around the corner of the eye wash station.

"Hey, you're all wet!"

Sam laughed as he reached down fondly to scratch Jet behind his ear.

Laverne tried not to fall out of her hiding place as she was buffed and jostled by the friendly rub. Hearing Sam say "taking off" made her think again of trying to fly and she yearned to stretch her wings. But that would have to wait for now. She felt herself slipping but she grasped the edge of Jet's ear fur with her tiny beak. Jet winced and let out a surprised yip.

"Sorry, boy, but this adventure requires the carrier again," said Sam as he placed the carrier on the ground and knelt down to encourage Jet to get in.

Sam was surprised how willing Jet was to enter his carrier. He usually showed his disappointment by refusing for a bit before walking in with his tail hanging low.

Jet got in the carrier just as Laverne fell out.

"Kee-ZINK!" she blurted as she landed with a thud inside the carrier.

"What was that you said, boy?" Sam puzzled. "For a minute there, you sounded like a bird!" Sam laughed.

"If you only knew!" thought Jet, as he shielded his stowaway. He was really getting worried that he would not be able to help his new friend get back to her family.

"Maybe he's practicing another language so he can talk to some new friends today," Mayra said as she came around the corner with the whole gang. "Quick, let's get in the van and get on the airfield!"

"Airfield?" thought Jet. "Hey, this just might work!"

Pearl hummed a tune as Mayra swiped her badge and escorted the Airport Explorers onto the airfield. They gathered around the van parked near the runway and Sam helped Mayra load the strange boxes of equipment and the canine carrier into the back. Jet heard something rattling around in one of the equipment boxes next to his carrier. "What's that funny clinky sound coming from the box?" thought Jet.

Over the roar of planes, Pete spoke up. "Tell us more about today's mission, Mayra!" he shouted.

Jet was all ears. Perhaps he could use Mayra's information to make a plan to get Laverne back to her nest at the end of the runway. The gang was on an environmental mission, Laverne's mission was to fly, and Jet knew that his personal mission was to get his new friend safely home.

"Buckle up everyone! Today we will be putting on tracking bracelets," explained Mayra.

"Ooh, I love jewelry!" grinned Pearl as she snapped her seatbelt.

"Oh, *that's* the clinky, clink," thought Jet.

Mayra continued, "The bracelets aren't for us, Pearl. They're for the least terns, so we can track where they go and what they do. It helps us keep them safe here at San Diego International Airport."

LEAST TERNS?!? Jet and Laverne both were so startled they bumped into each other in the carrier and fell over. As they regained their balance, they looked into each other's eyes. Could this be? Could Laverne be going home?

As the van motored along at a safe speed, Mayra continued.

"The airport protects the natural resources on and around the airport and in the surrounding community. We provide a protected habitat for the endangered California least terns here at the airport."

"I never heard of a bird called a least tern before," admitted Pete.

Mayra explained, "Its scientific name is Sterna antillarum browni."

Pete let out a low whistle. "That's a mouthful!" he said.

Mayra smiled and continued. "Basically, a least tern is a migrating seabird. One of the places they like to make their nests is along the southeastern property line of San Diego International Airport."

"What does 'migrating' mean, Mayra?" Sam wanted to know.

"To migrate means to take a journey from one place to another, to travel or transfer around," explained Mayra. "These birds come here in the spring. They lay their eggs in shallow nests on sand and gravel near the runway. On average a speckled least tern egg is a little over an inch long."

Pete was surprised. "Why would least terns want to nest by a noisy runway?"

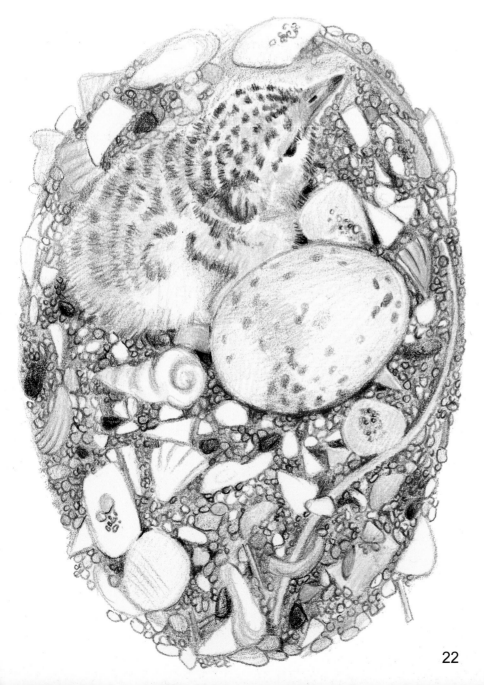

"Scientists have a theory that all the aircraft noise and commotion might scare the least terns' predators away. The terns may have been nesting in this area before the airport was built, and just decided to stay. Besides, the San Diego Bay is right next door."

"That's a constant food supply!" offered Sam.

"You've got it, Sam. New parents have to continually feed their new chicks. They fly over the bay every twenty to forty minutes to take a dip and catch some fish to bring back to their nests. They eat northern anchovy, jacksmelt, California killifish, walleye surfperch, shiner perch. . . ."

"And topsmelt!" whispered Laverne. Jet smiled.

"I'll bet their eggs are speckled for camouflage," said Pearl.

"That's right, Pearl. And the chicks' coloring, too. Their mixed colors blend in with their surrounding habitat of pebbles, sand, and dirt." said Mayra.

She continued. "We work hard to be good neighbors. Since they choose to put their nest so close to our runway, we protect their least tern chicks from wandering into danger."

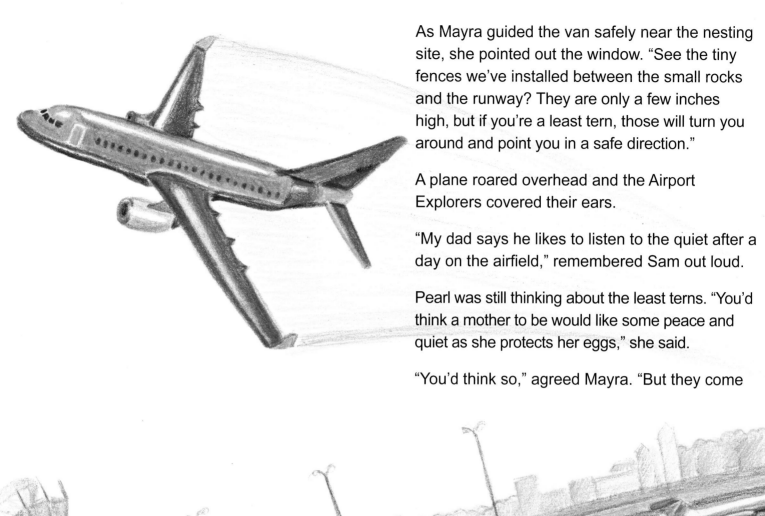

As Mayra guided the van safely near the nesting site, she pointed out the window. "See the tiny fences we've installed between the small rocks and the runway? They are only a few inches high, but if you're a least tern, those will turn you around and point you in a safe direction."

A plane roared overhead and the Airport Explorers covered their ears.

"My dad says he likes to listen to the quiet after a day on the airfield," remembered Sam out loud.

Pearl was still thinking about the least terns. "You'd think a mother to be would like some peace and quiet as she protects her eggs," she said.

"You'd think so," agreed Mayra. "But they come

to nest each year from spring through late summer, and the airport takes care of them. Protected nesting sites like ours have helped increase the numbers of least terns. They're on the endangered species list."

"Told ya," whispered Laverne.

As the van rolled along beside the runway, Mayra finished her story. "Least tern babies grow up fast. They reach full adult size in just three weeks! Once the chicks are ready to leave in late summer, the least terns will head to Mexico and other points south of San Diego's airport."

"Ready for take-off! Do they get clearance from the Air Traffic Control Tower?" joked Pete.

Everyone laughed. Mayra said, "I bet the guys in the tower would like that—we had almost a hundred and fifty nests last year!"

"So what ARE the bracelets for and what do they look like?" Pearl asked.

"That's what we're working on today. The bracelets are tracking devices that are placed onto a leg of each least tern that we spot. They are used by scientists to track the birds' age, growth, and birthplace. They are either silver or colored. The silver ones are only placed on the chicks. They each have an identification number on them to identify where and when the chicks were born. The colored plastic bracelets are placed only on the adult birds to let scientists know where the bird was last trapped and weighed."

"Hey," Laverne whispered to Jet. "Do you think that I can get one of those bracelets for my mom? It would make a great souvenir of my adventure!"

"I think getting you home will be treasure enough," smiled Jet. "But it sounds like your whole family will get bracelets if we find them!"

The van began to slow down. The Airport Explorers peered out the windows, each hoping to be the first to spot a nest, egg, or least tern.

Mayra brought the van to a complete stop. Jet began to whimper. He hoped that Sam would allow him to be on a leash to enjoy this adventure. His buddy Sam read his mind.

"Come on, boy," said Sam, as he opened the carrier and snapped on a leash. Laverne quickly slipped under a now-familiar ear and carefully held onto the warm soft fur.

The Airport Explorers piled out of the van with Mayra leading the way. They tiptoed carefully and kept their eyes wide open.

"Kee-ZINK! There's my nest!" shouted Laverne with excitement. The shout made Jet jump in his tracks.

"Quiet, Jet! I heard one," said Pete softly.

"Yeah, so did I!" thought Jet, his ear still throbbing from Laverne's outburst.

"Right over there," said Laverne more quietly as she tugged to one side of her furry hideaway.

Jet strained on the leash to get Sam's attention.

"Do you see something, boy?" Sam asked.

All eyes focused on the direction Jet was pulling. Laverne used the diversion to crawl around Jet's collar and perch on top of his head for a better view. The first thing she saw was a sad-looking adult least tern, wandering alone near her nest.

"Mommy!" Laverne chirped.

Suddenly, without thinking about it, Laverne took flight. She soared up into the air and spread her wings. She dipped her head and curved gracefully as her feathers cut through the air.

"Look at me!" Laverne exclaimed. Her mom looked up and saw her in flight. So did Jet, who smiled and wagged his tail.

"Mission accomplished!" he thought to himself.

"I see a least tern!" Sam shouted.

"Oh that's a young one," Mayra said looking as Laverne swooped by. "She's just learned to fly."

Mayra emptied her boxes. She began to carefully find and pick up terns for tagging.

Laverne landed safely and proudly beside her home and rubbed her soft head on her mother's wing. "Your dad will be so proud of you," Laverne's mom told her. "Where have you been?"

"Getting you a souvenir," Laverne told her mother with a smirk.

28

Jet took that as a cue to carefully lead the Airport Explorers and Mayra over to the nest, just as Laverne's dad circled overhead and glided in.

"Look, a whole family!" said a delighted Mayra, as she stepped lightly toward the least terns.

"Kee-ZINK! Predators!" squawked Laverne's defiant dad as he lifted his wings and prepared to safeguard his home.

"Don't worry, Dad. They're my friends. Especially this one," Laverne beamed as she flapped her wings, rose swiftly into the air, and landed squarely on Jet's forehead.

"Looks like you made a new buddy, Jet!" said Pete.

"More than you know," thought Jet, as he wagged his tail.

"They brought us bracelets as souvenirs," Laverne explained to her folks, as Mayra delicately picked up Laverne's mother and placed a colored band on her leg.

"Wow, usually we can only catch the chicks that can't fly yet!" whispered Mayra, as she prepared to weigh the bird and make some notes.

"That used to be me," Laverne said proudly as she flew over to Mayra and tickled her with her feathers.

"Hey, you're a friendly one," smiled Mayra as she snapped a shiny silver band onto Laverne's leg. Laverne held it out for Jet to admire.

"Come on, Dad. Your turn," instructed Laverne.

The protective father warily approached Mayra, who placed a colored band around his leg.

"This has been an amazing day!" declared Mayra, as she logged information about all three bracelet recipients into her scientific notes. "But we should be getting back."

"It sure has been an amazing day," thought Jet. He was a little sad, knowing it was time to say goodbye to his new friend. At first he thought Laverne would somehow get him in trouble, but all he'd had was crazy fun since he'd met Laverne, and he knew he would miss her terribly.

Jet's tail hung low and his ears began to droop. Still, he knew everyone had accomplished their missions on this incredible adventure, and that felt good.

"I'll miss you, Jet," Laverne chirped bravely. It was about all she could say without letting the tears in her eyes drop.

"I'll miss you, too, Sterna antillarum browni. I'm proud of you. Keep on flying." Jet was trying to sound more cheerful than he really was feeling.

"I'm working on it, thanks to you," she smiled back.

"Don't be sad, Jet," said Mayra, noticing his glum appearance. "You'll get the chance to visit your new friend before she migrates. We come out to visit the nests about twice a week to check on the least terns."

With that, Jet wagged his tail. His ears perked to attention. His eyes lit up.

Sam gave Jet a BIG hug. "That's my boy," he said.

The Airport Explorers grabbed their backpacks and Mayra gathered her equipment. As they headed toward the van, Jet looked back at Laverne.

"Mission accomplished," he winked. "See you soon."

Sam grabbed his backpack. "Hey, what happened to my peanut butter sandwich?"

"Kee-ZINK!" thought Jet and Laverne at the same time.

31

www.airportexplorers.com

Enjoy aviation fun,
games, activity pages, and more!

Teachers and parents—download free curriculum resources.

Purchase your own plush toy of **Laverne** today!

San Diego International Airport (SDIA) is proud to provide a protected nesting habitat for the California least tern, a federally listed endangered species.

For more on SDIA's environmental efforts and the California least tern, visit

san.org

The Airport Explorers™ is a trademark of the Aviation Education Program at San Diego International Airport.

The mission of San Diego County Regional Airport Authority's Airport Explorers™ program is to provide educational opportunities that give children of all ages inspiration to reach for the sky; foster understanding and appreciation for the extraordinary aviation achievements of the past; satisfy curiosity and interest in current and future airport operations; and cultivate dreams of flight that inspire future flyers to take wing.